EXTREMELY CURIOUS
Questions and Answers

EXTREMELY
CURIOUS
Questions and Answers

Words by Ian Graham, Anne Rooney and Camilla de la Bédoyère

Illustrations by Genie Espinosa (cover), Barbara Bakos, Pauline Reeves, Daniel Rieley and Tim Budgen

MILES KELLY

First published in 2019 by Miles Kelly Publishing Ltd
Harding's Barn, Bardfield End Green, Thaxted, Essex, CM6 3PX, UK

Copyright © Miles Kelly Publishing Ltd 2019

2 4 6 8 10 9 7 5 3 1

Publishing Director Belinda Gallagher
Creative Director Jo Cowan
Editorial Director Rosie Neave
Senior Editor Amy Johnson
Designers Rob Hale, Joe Jones, Simon Lee
Image Manager Liberty Newton
Production Elizabeth Collins, Jennifer Brunwin-Jones
Reprographics Stephan Davis, Callum Ratcliffe-Bingham
Assets Lorraine King

ISBN 978-1-78617-940-1

Printed in China

British Library Cataloguing-in-Publication Data
A catalogue record for this book is available from the British Library

Made with paper from a sustainable forest

www.mileskelly.net

CONTENTS

SOLAR SYSTEM 10

SCIENCE 42

OUR PLANET 74

OCEANS 106

Index 138

Where is the Solar System?

It's all around you. The Solar System is the Sun, eight planets and everything else that moves through space with the Sun.

The planet we live on is called Earth. It's the third planet from the Sun.

Earth

Sun
In the middle of the Solar System is a star called the Sun.

Venus

Mercury

Moons
A moon is a small world that circles a bigger object – usually a planet. Earth has one, and it is made of rock.

Planets
Planets are the giant things like the Earth that travel round the Sun. There are eight in our Solar System.

The four planets closest to the Sun are small worlds made mostly of rock.

How do you make a solar system?

Our Solar System began as a huge cloud of gas and dust in space.

①

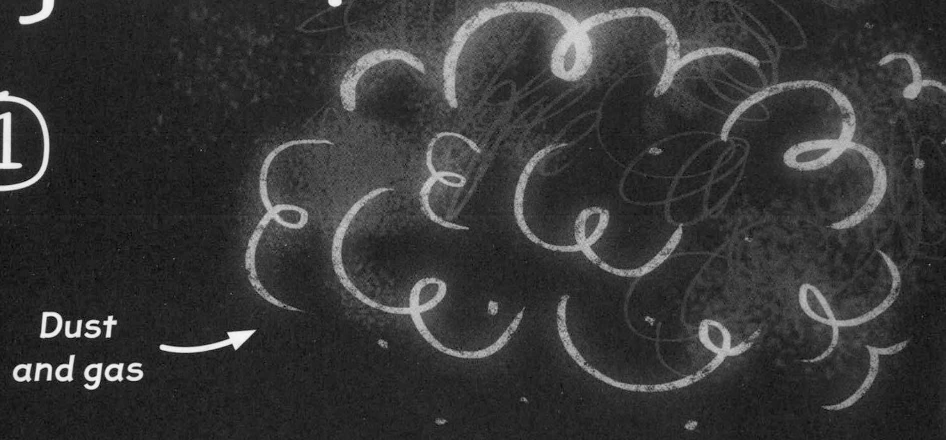

Dust and gas →

How did the Solar System begin, and where did it come from?

First, an exploding star pushed against the cloud. The whole dusty cloud began to shrink.

③

So, there was a swirling disc of dust and gas – then what happened?

The dust and gas began to stick together, forming lumps that smashed into each other.

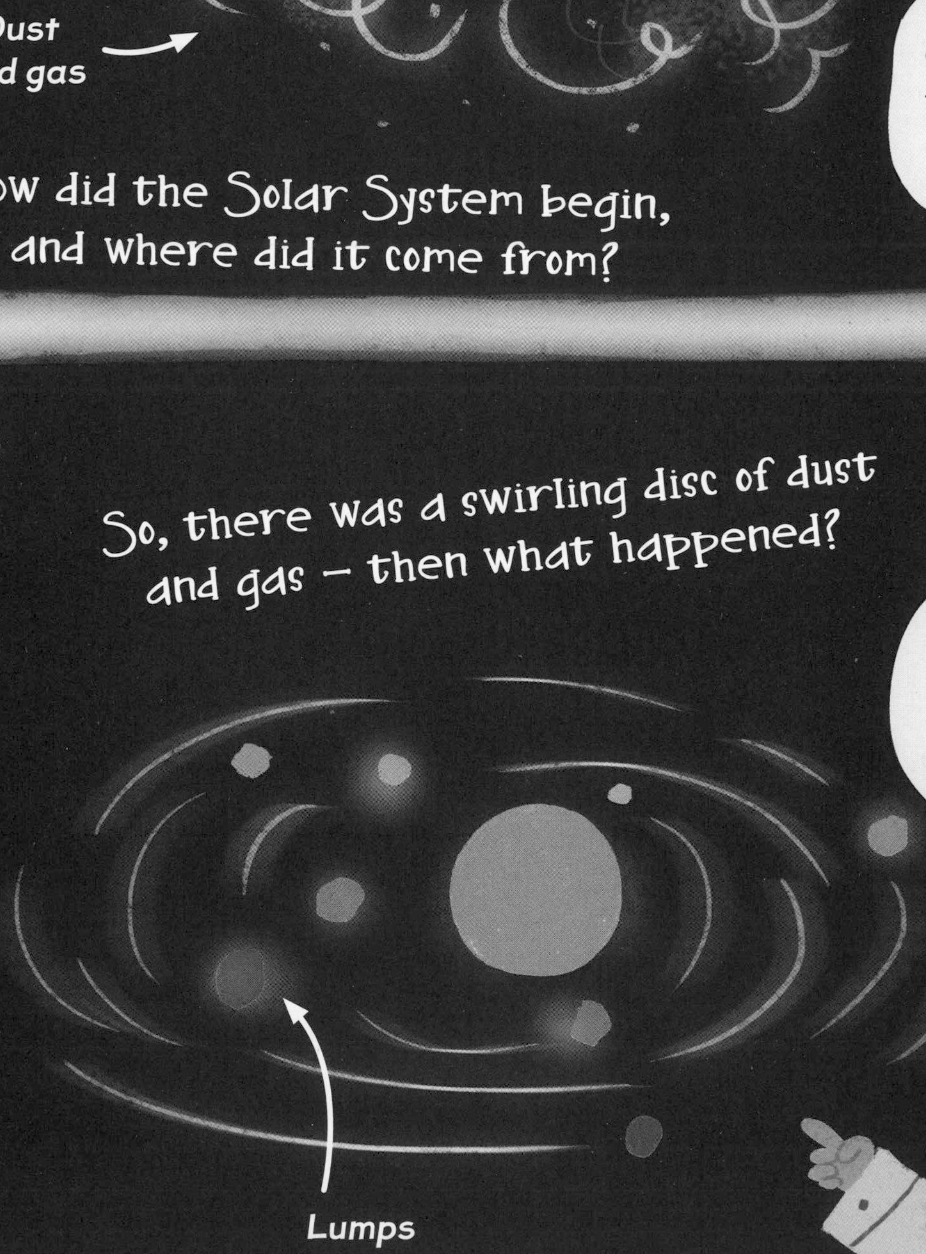

Lumps

Is the Sun hotter than an oven?

The Sun's surface is over 20 times hotter than a regular oven! The centre is even hotter – thousands of times hotter than an oven. It would melt the oven!

Surface

Core

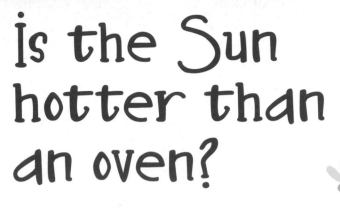

NEVER NEVER look at the Sun. It's so bright and hot that it will hurt your eyes.

HYDROGEN

HELIUM

What is the Sun made of?

It's mostly made of stuff called hydrogen and helium. On Earth, hydrogen and helium are gases.

Why is the Sun bigger than other stars?

It isn't – the Sun is actually a small star. It looks much bigger than the other stars you see at night, because it is much closer to Earth than those other stars. They're all suns, but they are very far away.

Side-by-side with another star, I'm actually pretty tiny!

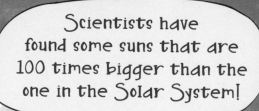

Scientists have found some suns that are 100 times bigger than the one in the Solar System!

Will the Sun be there forever?

No, but don't worry – it isn't going to disappear any time soon. The Sun should be there for another 5000 million years.

Where does the Sun go at night?

The Sun doesn't go anywhere – it's the Earth that is moving!

Our planet spins around an invisible line called the axis. It's daytime for you when the side you live on faces the Sun.

This spinning motion makes it look to us on Earth as if the Sun rises in the morning, crosses the sky, and then disappears at sunset.

Light rays

Axis

N

S

Sunset

ZZZ

Why is a day 24 hours long?

It takes 24 hours for Earth to spin around once, and we call this a day.

Why do we have seasons?

Because Earth's axis is tilted. This means different bits of Earth get the Sun's direct rays at different times during Earth's orbit (journey around the Sun).

What is the Equator?

It's an invisible line that circles Earth. It divides it into a northern (top) half and southern (bottom) half.

Equator

In June, it's summer in the north and winter in the south.

In March, it's spring in the north, and autumn in the south.

N
S

In December, it's winter in the north and summer in the south.

In September, it's autumn in the north and spring in the south.

What is a year?

A year is the time it takes for the Earth to complete one orbit of the Sun.

Did you know?

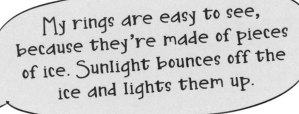

Jupiter has a huge storm called the Great Red Spot – it's about three times bigger than **Earth**.

Neptune is the Solar System's windiest planet, with winds ten times faster than the worst hurricanes on **Earth**.

Saturn is famous for its rings, but **Jupiter**, **Uranus** and **Neptune** have them too.

My rings are easy to see, because they're made of pieces of ice. Sunlight bounces off the ice and lights them up.

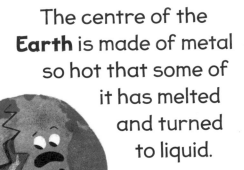

Our rings are thin, dark and dusty so they're hard to see.

The centre of the **Earth** is made of metal so hot that some of it has melted and turned to liquid.

You can jump six times higher on the **Moon** than you can on **Earth**.

Jupiter's moon **Ganymede** is the biggest moon in the Solar System – even bigger than the planet **Mercury**.

Dust storms are common on **Mars**. The sky there is pinky red, as so much red dust is blown about by the wind.

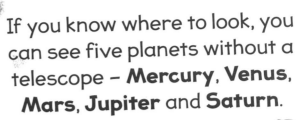

If you know where to look, you can see five planets without a telescope – **Mercury**, **Venus**, **Mars**, **Jupiter** and **Saturn**.

They are so far away they look like stars.

I'm only about half the width of the USA!

Astronauts who visited the **Moon** brought 382 kilograms of Moon rocks back with them.

Pluto was the Solar System's ninth planet – until 2006 when scientists decided to call it a dwarf planet instead.

There are between two and five solar eclipses every year.

Giant **Jupiter** spins so fast it has the shortest day of any planet – just 9 hours 55 minutes.

A solar eclipse happens when the **Moon** passes in front of the **Sun**. The Moon's shadow then moves across **Earth**, causing darkness to fall.

Are other planets like Earth?

Earth and the other three planets closest to the Sun are alike in some ways, but no other planet is exactly like Earth.

Why is it always so hot here?

Mercury is very hot because it's the closest planet to the Sun. It's smaller than Earth and it looks like the Moon.

Mercury

Why am I known as Earth's twin planet?

Venus

Venus and Earth are similar in size and structure – but the two planets look very different. Venus is wrapped in thick clouds of acid. They trap heat, so Venus is even hotter than Mercury.

What are the outer planets like?

The four planets farthest from the Sun – Jupiter, Saturn, Uranus and Neptune – couldn't be more different from Earth. They are giant worlds made of gas and liquid.

Jupiter

Saturn

Where did my rings come from?

How big am I?

Jupiter is the biggest planet in the Solar System. It's so big that more than a thousand Earths would fit inside it!

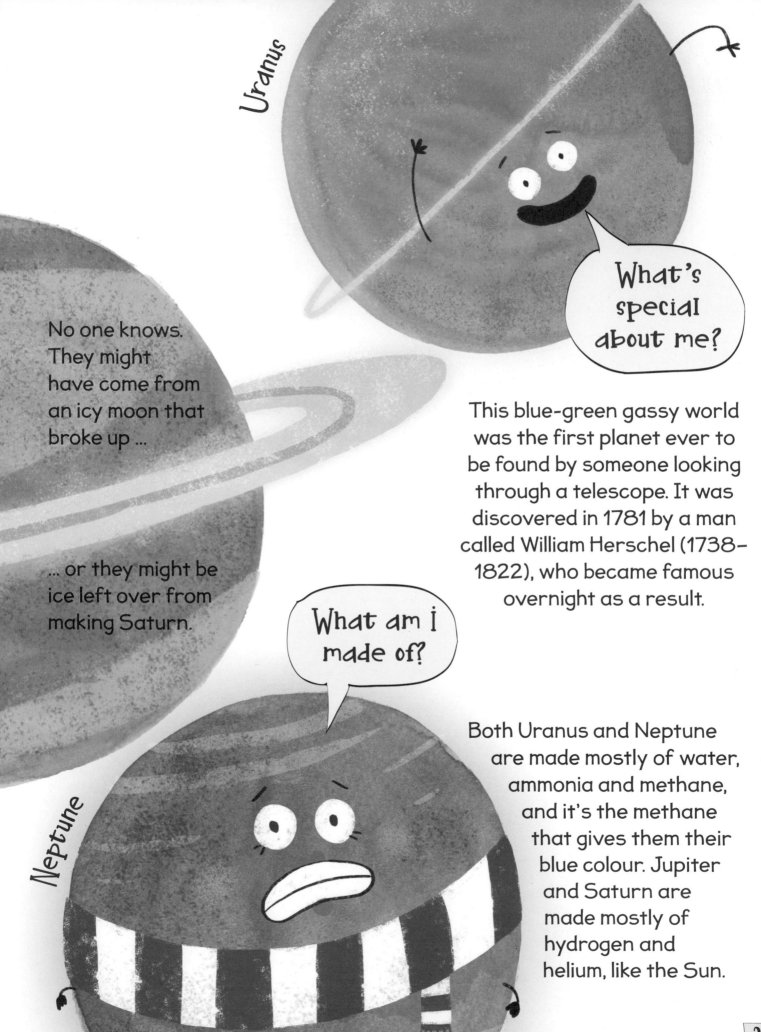

Uranus

No one knows. They might have come from an icy moon that broke up ...

... or they might be ice left over from making Saturn.

What's special about me?

This blue-green gassy world was the first planet ever to be found by someone looking through a telescope. It was discovered in 1781 by a man called William Herschel (1738–1822), who became famous overnight as a result.

What am I made of?

Neptune

Both Uranus and Neptune are made mostly of water, ammonia and methane, and it's the methane that gives them their blue colour. Jupiter and Saturn are made mostly of hydrogen and helium, like the Sun.

Do planets ever crash into each other?

Almost never. Billions of years ago, a planet the size of Mars crashed into Earth and sent lots of rock flying out into space. Can you guess what happened next?

① A planet called Theia crashed into Earth.

② The crash threw lots of rocks into space around Earth.

③ The rocks in space came together and became the Moon.

The Moon is the only place beyond Earth that humans have set foot on.

What's it like on the Moon?

The Moon is very dry and covered with grey dust. There are mountains, but there is no air, and the sky is always inky black.

Why is the Moon covered with craters?

These dents are made when rocks flying through space hit the Moon.

④ The Moon travels through space at a distance of 384,400 kilometres from Earth. Every year the Moon moves 4 centimetres further away from Earth.

Would you rather?

Would you rather discover a new planet, like **William Herschel** did...

...or work out that all the planets in the Solar System orbit the Sun, like **Nicolaus Copernicus** did?

Would you rather live on **Earth** for your whole life, or spend your whole life in a **space station** where you could float about weightless?

If I lived on Mercury I'd be sixteen!

If I lived on Neptune I'd be younger than you!

Would you rather kick a ball really far on the **Moon** or make a red sandcastle on **Mars**?

Would you prefer to live on **Mercury**, where a year lasts just 88 Earth days, or on **Neptune**, where a year lasts 165 Earth years?

Which part of astronaut training would you rather do:

Work in a huge tank of water to practise **space walks**...

...or take a spin to get a feel for **extreme forces**?

If you had to name a new planet, would you rather call it **Aether**, after the Greek god of light, or **Erebus**, the god of darkness?

On a space mission, would you rather be the **pilot** flying the spacecraft, or a **specialist**, doing experiments and going on space walks?

Would you rather live on Uranus in **winter**, when the Sun doesn't rise for 20 years, or in **summer**, when it doesn't set for 20 years?

Would you rather slow down **Earth's** spin so days are longer, or move Earth closer to the **Sun** so that the weather is warmer?

What are shooting stars?

They're not stars! They're small pieces of rock that fly through space and into the air around Earth. Rubbing against the air heats them until they glow. They are also called meteors.

When lots of meteors appear in the sky, it's called a meteor shower.

Where do shooting stars go?

The smallest burn up and disappear. Others sometimes fall all the way down to the ground. If they land on Earth, they're called meteorites.

What happens when a big meteorite hits Earth?

It makes a hole in the ground called a crater. A famous crater in Arizona, USA, was made by a meteorite 50 metres across that hit the ground 50,000 years ago.

Why do comets have long, bright tails?

Comets are like giant dusty snowballs in space. If they fly near the Sun, some of the ice turns to gas and bursts out, carrying dust with it. The dust forms a tail that is lit up by sunlight.

How big are space rocks?

The biggest rocks in space are asteroids. Some can be up to 1000 kilometres across. Most asteroids are found in the Asteroid Belt between Mars and Jupiter.

How many?

-200° Celsius:

Brrrrrrrrr!

The average temperature on the Solar System's coldest planet, Neptune.

178 moons have been found going around planets so far. More might be found in future.

Life appeared on Earth about **4,000,000,000** years ago.

7,500,000,000: The number of people living on Earth.

0 The number of moons that the planets Mercury and Venus have.

The Solar System is about **4,600,000,000** years old.

The Solar System's tallest mountain is Olympus Mons on Mars. It's nearly **3** times the height of the tallest mountain on Earth, Mount Everest.

How many astronauts have walked on the Moon?

12

The Sun is so big that **109** Earths would fit side by side across its middle.

150 million kilometres: the distance from Earth to the Sun.

Halley's Comet appears in the sky every

76

years.

Just over **8** minutes: the amount of time it takes for sunlight to reach Earth.

165

The number of Earth years it takes the farthest planet, Neptune, to go once around the Sun.

3

...the number of days it takes astronauts to fly to the Moon in a spacecraft.

There are **5** dwarf planets in the Solar System. They are called...

Eris

Pluto

Haumea

Makemake

Ceres

How do we know about other planets?

No human has ever visited another planet, but we learn about them by sending robot spacecraft to study them. We have sent more spacecraft to Mars than any other planet.

Solar panels provide power

Robotic arm

I used my robotic arm to scoop up Martian soil to find out what it's made of.

Phoenix lander

Do spacecraft land on other planets?

Yes! Spacecraft that land on a planet are called landers. They take photographs of the surface and measure things like the temperature and wind speed. A spacecraft called Phoenix landed on Mars in 2008.

Mars Reconnaissance Orbiter

Powerful camera

How do we get good photos of Mars?

Robot spacecraft like me are called orbiters. We fly round and round it, like tiny moons. As we circle, we take photos and send them back to Earth by radio.

What is a rover?

Some of the spacecraft on Mars have wheels so that they can move around and explore more of the planet. They're called rovers. A rover called Curiosity landed on Mars in 2012.

My mission is to investigate Martian climate and geology, to find out whether Mars can support any life.

Special instruments measure temperatures, wind speeds, radiation, and much more

Curiosity

Is there life anywhere else?

Not that we know of – the search goes on. The spacecraft we have sent to other planets have been searching for signs of life there.

Erm... hello? Is anyone at home?

Why is there life on Earth?

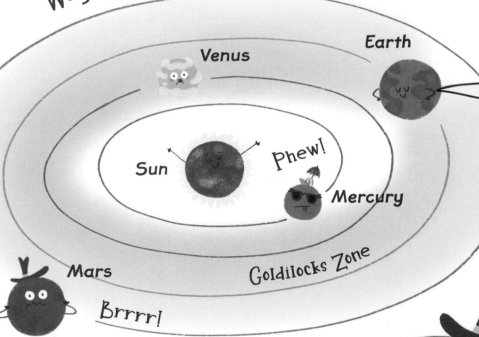

Venus

Earth

Sun

Phew!

Mercury

Mars

Goldilocks Zone

Brrrr!

My distance from the Sun means I have light, water and the correct temperature for life. I'm in what's called the 'Goldilocks Zone' – it's just right.

Why did people think aliens lived on Mars?

When people first used telescopes to study Mars they thought they saw lines on its surface. The idea spread that these were canals, made by aliens.

When spacecraft visited Mars, they found a dry, dusty planet with no canals – or aliens.

Is there water anywhere else in the Solar System?

Scientists think there may be oceans beneath the surfaces of some of Jupiter and Saturn's icy moons. Future missions will search for life there.

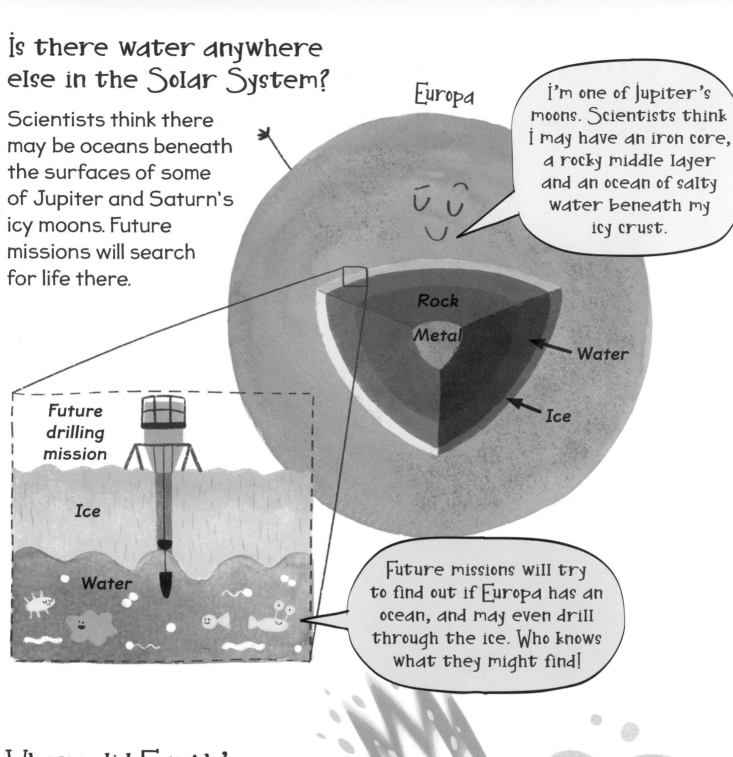

Europa

I'm one of Jupiter's moons. Scientists think I may have an iron core, a rocky middle layer and an ocean of salty water beneath my icy crust.

Rock

Metal

Water

Ice

Future drilling mission

Ice

Water

Future missions will try to find out if Europa has an ocean, and may even drill through the ice. Who knows what they might find!

Where did Earth's water come from?

Some of it was already in the rocks that formed the Earth. The rest arrived as ice on comets and other space rocks that crashed into Earth soon after it formed.

A compendium of questions

Pleased to meet you!

Why is Earth called Earth?

It comes from an ancient word meaning land. Earth is the only planet that wasn't named after an ancient Greek or Roman god.

Which moon is the weirdest?

Hmmm... maybe Saturn's moon Enceladus. It spews jets of gas and ice from its south pole!

The jets come from an ocean of water beneath Enceladus' icy surface

Are there rainbows on the Moon?

Sunlight and rain are both needed for a rainbow. There is no rain on the Moon, so you will never see a rainbow there.

Why is the Earth's sky blue?

As sunlight travels through air, the blue part of the light is scattered in all directions, so the sky looks blue.

Where is the best view of the Sun?

Standing on Mercury when it is at its closest to the Sun, the Sun would appear more than three times as large as it does from Earth.

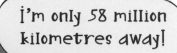

I'm only 58 million kilometres away!

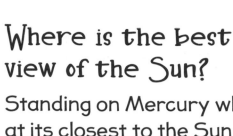

Why aren't planets square?

Planets are round because of gravity. This special force pulls everything inwards, forming a ball shape.

Is there lightning on other planets?

Yes. Spacecraft have seen lightning storms on Venus, Jupiter and Saturn.

Can a spacecraft land on a gas planet?

Scientists think Jupiter's core could be up to 50,000° Celsius! Phew!

No – and they can't fly through them either! The extreme temperature and pressure inside would crush a spacecraft.

Why are the planets different colours?
Because planets are made of different mixtures of rocks and gases that reflect light in different ways.

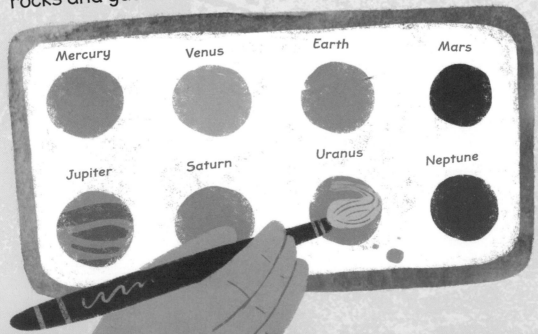

Mercury   Venus   Earth   Mars

Jupiter   Saturn   Uranus   Neptune

Who is the Man in the Moon?

Some people think marks on the surface look like a face. Others think they can see the shape of a rabbit.

When did the first spacecraft go to the Moon?

In 1959, Luna 2 became the first spacecraft to crash-land there – no astronauts were onboard.

Are all the stars part of our Solar System?

No – the Sun is our only star. All the others are outside our Solar System.

Many other stars have their own families of planets.

Why do the planets spin?

The giant cloud of dust and gas that formed the Solar System started spinning as it shrank. The planets that formed from it carried on spinning.

Science

How do we find things out?

We know about the world around us because scientists look carefully and carry out experiments. You could be a scientist! All you have to do is...

① Spot a problem

Keep your eyes and ears open. Look out for questions to ask and problems to solve.

② Have an idea

Think of something that could explain or solve the problem. This is your theory.

③ Design an experiment

Work out how to test your idea – an experiment. Change just one thing at a time to make a fair test.

④ Check what happens

Were you right? If not, you might need a new theory and a new experiment.

① Long ago, sailors were often ill with a disease called scurvy.

These long journeys are killing me! Can't somebody do something?

② Scientist James Lind (1716–1794) decided to investigate.

I think it might be what you're eating – or what you're not eating.

Cider

Oranges and lemons

Sea water

It's worth a try...

Vinegar

Lind chose six pairs of sick sailors. All had the same food, except he gave each pair one extra thing.

Months later, the sailors who had oranges and lemons were better. The rest were even more sick.

I want what he had!

Why do we need scientists?

The work of scientists can make life better. A discovery can lead to more questions and experiments. Science keeps on going.

Modern scientists found out that it is the Vitamin C in fruit that stops scurvy.

Do plants eat?

Plants don't eat like animals do – they use sunlight to make their own food in their leaves.

Sunflower

All living things need energy. We get ours from sunlight. We use this energy to turn water and gas into food.

I can't grow in the shade, as I'm not getting the sunlight I need.

Plants don't breathe like you, but gases go in and out through their leaves.

Sunlight acts on chemicals in the plant's leaves to make food.

Secondary roots

Main root

What use are roots?

Roots keep plants fixed in the soil so they don't fall over or blow away! Through their roots, plants take in water and small amounts of chemicals from the soil. Roots also store food for the plant.

How are new plants made?

Most plants reproduce – make baby plants – by producing seeds.

The seeds fall to the ground, blow away in the wind, or are spread by animals to new places to grow.

Dandelion seeds

Dandelion

Some plants make fruit with seeds in. Animals eat the fruit. The seeds come out in their poo, ready to grow somewhere else.

Parent strawberry plant

Runner

New strawberry plant

Certain types of plants grow baby plants on special stalks called runners. The new plants then grow their own roots and the runner drops off.

How many?

320

The number of days it would take to drive to the Moon non-stop at 50 kilometres per hour.

60–70

The percentage of your body that is water.

300,000,000

The speed in metres per second that light travels.

3%

How much taller an astronaut is in space where gravity is not pulling their body downwards.

50%

The proportion of cells in your body that are not you, but germs and other micro organisms.

A skydiver can reach a speed of **195** kilometres per hour.

1,000,000,000,000,000,000,000,000

Roughly how many stars there are in the known Universe.

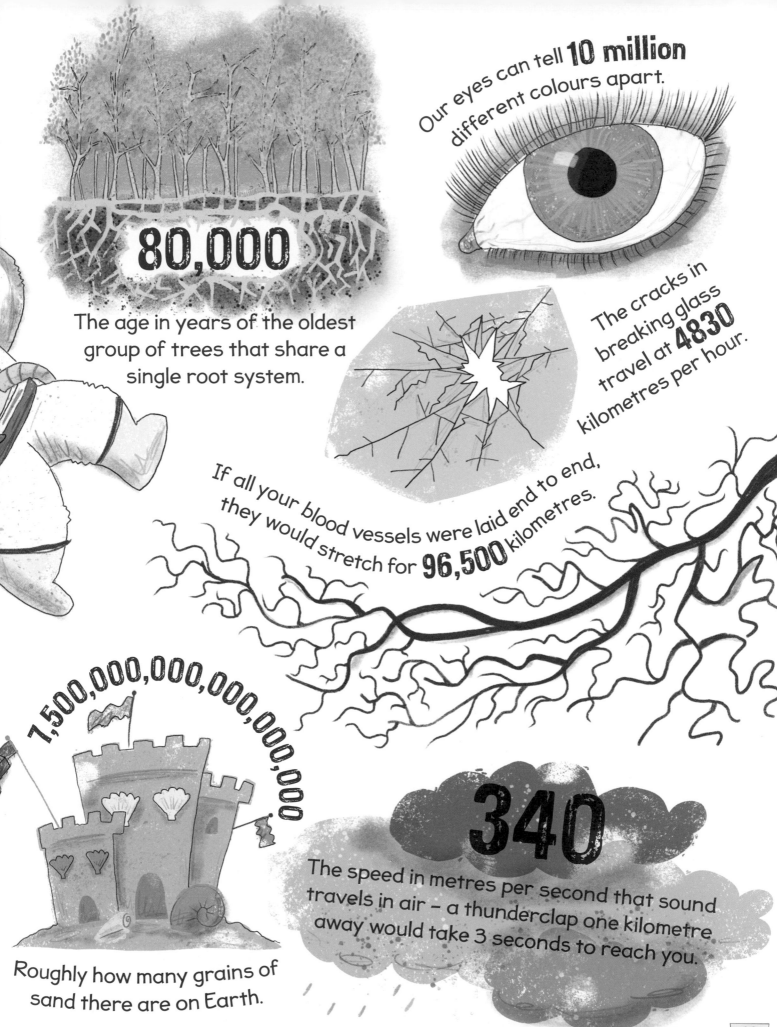

80,000

The age in years of the oldest group of trees that share a single root system.

Our eyes can tell **10 million** different colours apart.

The cracks in breaking glass travel at **4830** kilometres per hour.

If all your blood vessels were laid end to end, they would stretch for **96,500** kilometres.

1,500,000,000,000,000,000,000

Roughly how many grains of sand there are on Earth.

340

The speed in metres per second that sound travels in air – a thunderclap one kilometre away would take 3 seconds to reach you.

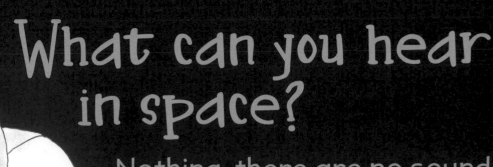

What can you hear in space?

Nothing, there are no sounds in space. Sound travels as vibrations through matter. As space is empty, there is nothing for sound to travel through.

> I can hear noises inside my suit and in my headset but not from outside. Anything could sneak up on me!

> Dolphins can hear much higher sounds than humans!

Why do things sound different underwater?

The vibrations are going through water, not air, making things sound a bit different. We can hear higher sounds in water than in air.

> Dolphins use sound to hunt for food and find their way underwater. They make noises such as clicks and buzzes.

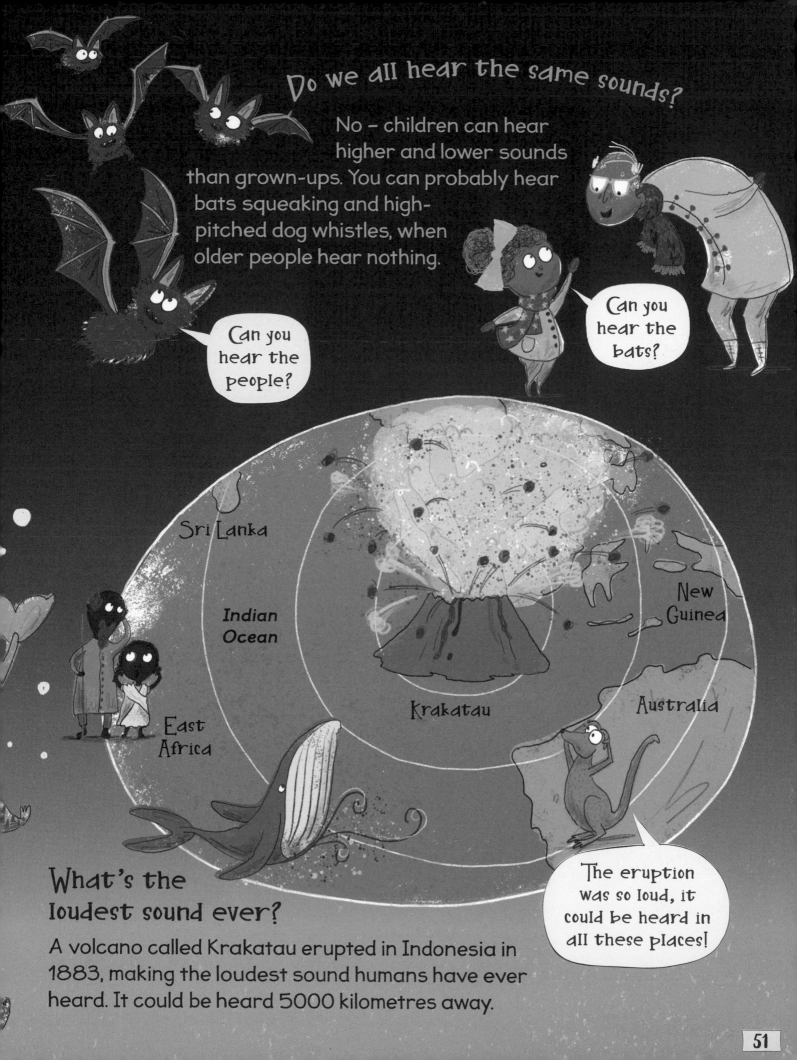

Do we all hear the same sounds?

No – children can hear higher and lower sounds than grown-ups. You can probably hear bats squeaking and high-pitched dog whistles, when older people hear nothing.

Can you hear the people?

Can you hear the bats?

Sri Lanka

Indian Ocean

New Guinea

East Africa

Krakatau

Australia

What's the loudest sound ever?

A volcano called Krakatau erupted in Indonesia in 1883, making the loudest sound humans have ever heard. It could be heard 5000 kilometres away.

The eruption was so loud, it could be heard in all these places!

How does electricity get to my house?

Electricity is a type of energy. It is generated in power stations then carried along a network of cables, all the way to the wires and power points throughout your house.

Lots of things we use every day, such as lights and computers, are powered by electricity. It makes the fridge cold, and the heater hot!

Can you spot some other objects that need electricity to work?

How is electricity made?

We get electricity by changing other forms of energy such as sunlight, wind, moving water, or by burning coal, oil or gas.

Coal, oil and gas are known as fossil fuels, because they come from the remains of animals and plants that lived long ago. A lot of our energy comes from burning fossil fuels.

Wires inside the walls carry electricity to all the places it's needed. We plug electrical objects into sockets in the wall.

Fossil fuels will run out in the future, and burning them causes pollution. So people are trying to use more energy from sources that can't be used up.

Solar power

Energy from sunlight is captured in solar panels and changed into electricity.

Water power

The energy of water held by a dam is changed into electrical energy.

Wind power

Wind turbines change the wind's movement energy into electricity.

Why do I feel ill?

Many illnesses are caused by germs – tiny things too small to see. There are germs everywhere. Your body tries to keep them out, and is good at fighting them when they get in.

How does my body fight germs?

It makes special cells (tiny parts of your body) that attack germs and anything else that shouldn't be inside you.

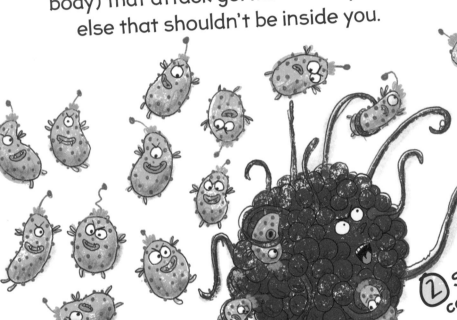

③ **They destroy the germs by swallowing them whole!**

② **Special body cells come to the rescue by attacking the germs.**

① **Once inside your body, germs set up home and start reproducing – soon there are lots and lots.**

What is a fever?

You might feel hot when you're ill. Your body pushes its temperature up to kill off germs that don't like the heat. This doesn't feel good, but it does you good!

Can I get the same type of germ again?

When you catch an illness like chickenpox, your body learns how to fight it. You probably won't get it again: if another chickenpox germ comes along, your body can deal with it quickly – it doesn't stand a chance.

While your body is fighting germs, you might feel ill. You might be sick, feel too hot, cough, sneeze or have aches and pains.

Did you know?

There are **meteorites** – tiny bits of rock from space – all around. One hits each square metre of ground about once a year.

Some **plants** eat insects and even small animals.

If you break a **magnet** in half, you get two magnets, each with a north and south pole.

If we could drill a hole right through the **Earth**, things wouldn't fall straight through; they would get to the middle and stop.

Nine tenths of an **iceberg** is under water. Ice only just floats, so not much sticks out.

If you put a **carnation** in coloured water, it will eventually suck up the water and turn the same colour.

Bamboo grows so fast you can watch it get taller. It can grow 91 centimetres in a single day.

If there was no air, a **feather** and **cricket ball** dropped from the same height would hit the ground together.

The **Apollo spacecraft** were landed on the Moon by a computer less powerful than a smartphone.

The largest land animal ever was **Patagotitan**, a dinosaur that weighed about 70 tonnes and was 37 metres long.

I weighed about the same as 12 African elephants!

Some **volcanic rocks** float on water. This is because they are full of air bubbles.

If you float a **needle** on water it lines up to point north/south.

Earth's continents move slowly all the time, so the **Atlantic Ocean** grows a few centimetres wider each year.

Why do I have a shadow?

Your body blocks light coming from the Sun or a lamp, making a darker patch on the other side.

Why is my reflection the wrong way round?

Light from the left side of your body travels to the mirror and bounces off, making the left side of your reflection.

If you were standing where your reflection is, that would be your right side, so it looks the wrong way round.

What makes a rainbow?

If sunlight (white light) passes through raindrops at the right angle, it is split up into a spectrum of colours inside the raindrops. The colours come out in different directions.

You see one colour from each raindrop – which colour depends on the angle you are looking at the raindrop. All together they make stripes – a rainbow!

Red
Orange
Yellow
Green
Blue
Indigo
Violet

Why can't I see round corners?

Light always travels in straight lines. You can see round corners, but only if you bounce the light around a bit using mirrors. This is how a periscope in a submarine works.

Mirror

Light

Mirror

What eats lions?

A few things nibble lions – like biting insects – and crocodiles sometimes kill lions. But mostly lions eat other animals. The world is full of creatures that eat each other.

How do animals make a chain?

The order in which animals eat each other – and plants – is called a food chain. It's easy to see who eats who.

Biting fly

Lion

Antelope

Grass

What do herbivores eat?

Herbivores are animals that eat plants. They can be big – like us giraffes – or tiny – like bugs and birds.

Most animals don't eat only one thing. Food chains fit together into a food web.

An omnivore is an animal that is able to eat both plants and other animals. Are you a carnivore, herbivore or omnivore?

Whose food is already dead?

Some creatures, such as vultures, eat carrion — animals that have already died. Vultures will eat the dead lion one day — and so will tiny bugs and worms.

What is a carnivore?

Carnivores are animals that eat other animals. Lions eat zebras, antelope and sometimes young giraffes.

Which animals help hippos?

These oxpeckers help me by eating the insects that bite my skin. This helps them because they get a good meal!

Why do things fall?

The force of gravity pulls objects towards the centre of the Earth – downwards! Gravity is everywhere in the Universe, pulling things with less mass towards things with more mass. The Earth has more mass than anything on it.

Things only move if a force acts on them. You can think of forces as 'pushes' or 'pulls'. I'm falling because gravity is pulling me down.

Gravity

Drag

Why does a parachute slow your fall?

A force called drag acts on the parachute. When the parachute opens, air is trapped under it. The air has to be pushed out of the way for the parachute to fall. The air holds the parachute up while gravity pulls it down.

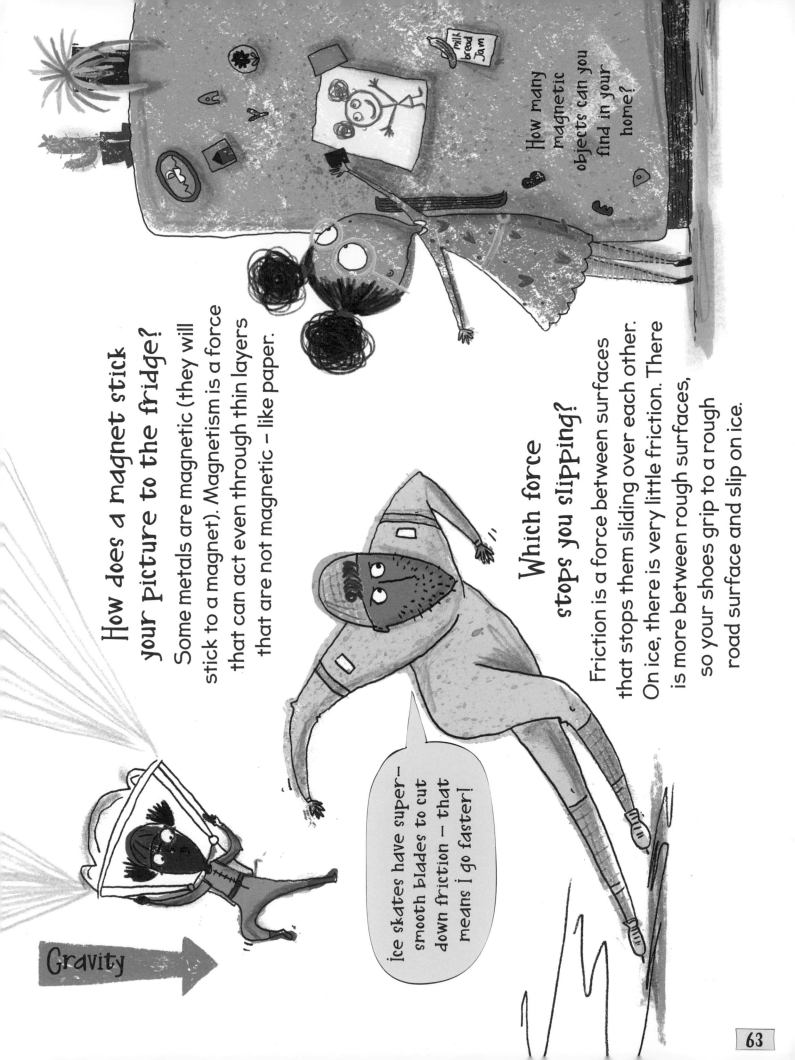

How does a magnet stick your picture to the fridge?

Some metals are magnetic (they will stick to a magnet). Magnetism is a force that can act even through thin layers that are not magnetic – like paper.

How many magnetic objects can you find in your home?

Which force stops you slipping?

Friction is a force between surfaces that stops them sliding over each other. On ice, there is very little friction. There is more between rough surfaces, so your shoes grip to a rough road surface and slip on ice.

Ice skates have super-smooth blades to cut down friction – that means I go faster!

Gravity

Would you rather?

Would you rather be a **vulture** that eats dead animals or a **worm** that eats soil?

If you were a superhero, would you rather have enough **friction** to walk up walls or be able to turn **gravity** off and float around?

Would it be better to be able to see **round corners** or in the **dark**?

Would you prefer to study **tigers** in the jungle or explore scary **volcanoes**?

Would you rather invent an amazing new **material** or design a fantastic **vehicle**?

Would you rather be **super-stretchy** like elastic, or **super-springy** and bounce everywhere?

Time for adventure! Would you rather be an **astronaut** going to Mars or a **diver** exploring the deepest oceans?

Would you rather be so **light** you can walk on water...

...or so **dense** you could walk along the seabed?

Gravity

A ship made of solid metal, without any air in it, would sink.

Buoyancy

Which force pushes up?

Buoyancy! Buoyancy is a force that pushes upwards through a fluid (such as water or air) against the weight of an object. When the weight pushing down (gravity) and the buoyancy are equal, the object doesn't move up or down.

Why do ships float?

Whether something sinks or floats depends on its density (how heavy something is for its volume). Most big ships are made of metal. Metal is more dense than water, but a ship floats because it is mostly full of air.

If we put in so much stuff the ship becomes denser than water, it will sink.

Do fish sink or float?

They can do both! Fish are almost the same density as water. Many types have a swim bladder, which is a sac filled with gas in their stomach. The amount of gas controls the fish's buoyancy to keep it at the right level in the water. It can add more gas to go up, or lose gas to go down.

What is matter?

Matter is everything around you! It has three states: a solid, a liquid, or a gas.

Solid
A solid (like paper, wood or plastic) can hold its shape.

Liquid
A liquid can't hold its shape. It spreads out into a pool unless it's held in a container.

Gas
A gas doesn't hold its shape. It spreads out as far as possible. To keep a gas in one place, we put it in a closed container.

The gas in my balloon can't get out.

Why does ice cream melt?

Materials change state as they heat up or cool down. Heating a solid above its melting point turns it to liquid. The melting point for ice cream is 0° Celsius.

To keep ice cream frozen solid, we store it in the freezer.

How does a liquid become a gas?

Heating a liquid to its boiling point turns it to a gas. The boiling point of water is 100° Celsius.

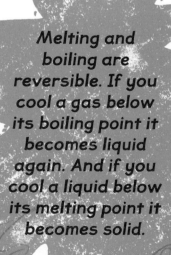

Melting and boiling are reversible. If you cool a gas below its boiling point it becomes liquid again. And if you cool a liquid below its melting point it becomes solid.

Not all things melt when heated – some just burn. Which of these things do you think would melt?

- Woolly sweater
- Egg
- Glass bottle
- Sausage
- Toffee
- Metal key
- Book
- Wooden chair

Answer:
glass, toffee and metal melt

A compendium of questions

Why is it cold at the North and South Poles?

The Earth is like a ball, so the top and bottom don't get much direct sunlight as they face away from the Sun.

Moon

Where do stars go in the daytime?

Nowhere! The light from the Sun is so bright that they just don't show up in daytime.

Why don't I freeze solid in icy weather?

You're warm-blooded, which means your body uses energy to keep you at a safe temperature.

What are shooting stars?

Meteorites – lumps of rock from space. They get so hot as they pass through the air above the Earth that they burn up, creating a streak of bright light.

Why does the tide go in and out?

The Moon's gravity pulls on the oceans. As the Earth turns, the water is pulled one way and then the other.

What is a cloud made of?

Tiny drops of water, so light that they are held up by the air. If too much water collects, the drops get heavier and fall as rain.

Why do I burp?

Food breaking down in your stomach makes gases. This collects in bubbles which come out at your top or bottom!

Why does a balloon go bang?
The air inside is under a lot of pressure. When the balloon bursts, air rushes out in a fast-moving wave. We hear this as a bang.

Is a bubble a solid, liquid or gas?
It is gas with a very thin skin of liquid around it.

Could astronauts go to the Sun?
No – the Sun is far too hot for any person or spaceship to survive getting close to.

Why are there no dinosaurs?
Dinosaurs and many other creatures all died out 65 million years ago by a natural disaster – probably a rock from space crashing into Earth.

At the South Pole, which way is up?

Towards the sky. Down is always towards the centre of the Earth. There is no up or down in space.

This way up!

Why isn't the world covered in poo?

Poo is eaten and broken down by dung beetles, worms and micro organisms. So poo is food for some things!

Can i be a scientist when i grow up?

Yes! Anyone can be a scientist – just stay curious!

What is the Earth?

The Earth is a big, blue planet that travels through space. It is the planet we live on – in fact it is full of life!

Polar bear

Animals and plants live on the land and in the oceans too!

Is there life on other planets?

Not that we know of. There are living things on Earth because there is air, water, warmth and light.

It's night time where the Earth faces away from the Sun.

Why is it dark at night?

As the Earth travels around the Sun it spins, too. This means sunlight can only shine on one part of the Earth at a time.

Penguin

South Pole

Is Earth like a jigsaw?

Yes, because it's made of pieces that fit together! The pieces are called plates and they are made of rock. The thickest parts of the plates poke up above the sea to form dry land, where we live.

The plates float on hot rock

The plates are always moving very slowly and creating new land, seas and mountains

How do mountains grow?

Mountains are the tallest parts of the planet. Most of them grow when one plate moves and crashes into another plate. The rocks bend and fold, making mountains.

When plates move they can create earthquakes and volcanoes

How tall is the tallest mountain?

Mount Everest is the tallest mountain, and it is 8848 metres high. Everest is part of a group of mountains called the Himalayas.

Bar-headed geese are some of the highest-flying birds. We can soar over the Himalayas.

Mountain goat

Mountains are millions of years old, but some of the rocks deep inside the Rocky Mountains could have been made more than a billion years ago!

Snow leopard

What lives on a mountain?

Nimble-footed snow leopards chase mountain goats across slippery slopes. Life is hard on a cold mountain because there is often snow all year round.

CRASH!

Moving plates smash together

Hot rock

How are rainbows made?

Although we can't see it, sunlight is made up of all the colours of the rainbow. As a beam of sunlight passes through raindrops, it is split into seven colours. This creates an arc of red, orange, yellow, green, blue, indigo and violet bands in the sky.

Sunlight has all the colours of the rainbow in it

Light enters raindrops

Light splits into seven colours

Each colour of light is bent a different amount as it passes through the raindrop.

The colours bend inside

The colours leave the raindrops and make a rainbow in the sky

Why does thunder clap?

In a thunderstorm, the loud noise you hear is actually caused by lightning. The air becomes so hot from the heat of electrical lightning, it expands very quickly, causing the sharp clapping or rumbling sound we call thunder.

Why is snow white?

Snow is made of lots of tiny ice crystals. When these crystals become packed together as snow on the ground, they reflect all the colours of light by the same amount. When this happens, white light is made, which is why snow appears white to us.

Snowflakes are made of ice crystals, and every one is different!

Did you know?

The loudest **thunderclaps** can shake houses and shatter glass windows.

More people have been to the **Moon** than have been to the deepest part of the **sea**.

If **Mount Everest** were at the bottom of the deepest ocean, its tip wouldn't appear above the water's surface!

The Earth's **plates** move very slowly – sometimes as little as 2 centimetres in one year.

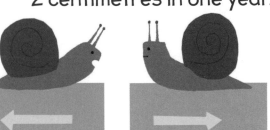

Bees can see colours in **sunlight** that are invisible to us, but they can't see red!

When **moonlight** is bright enough you might see a rainbow. It's called a **moonbow**.

Because of the way the world spins, you would weigh less if you were at the **North Pole** or **South Pole**!

If you took off in an **aeroplane** at breakfast time on Monday, and flew all around the world, you could be home for lunch on Wednesday!

We have just one **Sun**, but in outer space there are at least 200 billion more suns!

Huge piles of bat **poo** can collect in caves where bats sleep. The poo is so smelly that the gas it gives off can kill animals that want to move in.

The centre of the **Earth** is hotter than the surface of the Sun.

Big lumps of burning rock can explode out of a **volcano**, flattening anything they land on.

Planet Earth is a giant **magnet**. Animals such as bar-headed geese use the Earth's magnetism to find their way when they go on long journeys.

The mega-hot conditions deep inside a volcano make water boil so hard that layers of solid **gold** can form!

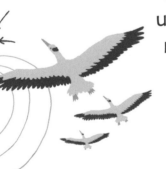

When the world's deepest lake **freezes** the ice can be more than one metre deep. Cars can drive on it!

The Andes are the longest chain of **mountains** in the world. They pass through seven countries!

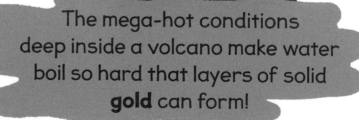

What is the water cycle?

The way that water moves around our planet is called the water cycle. Most of the world's water is salty.

Sun

Clouds start to form

Water vapour rises

Water is all around us, even when we can't see it. It's not just in the sea and rivers. It's also in the air and in the ground.

Salty water in the ocean warms up and turns into water vapour, a type of gas. This is called evaporation. The salt stays in the ocean.

People use fresh water to drink, cook, wash, grow their crops and give to their animals.

Water vapour cools and turns to liquid water and falls as rain or snow. It is freshwater, which means we can drink it.

Some water flows through the ground

Water flows downhill, in rivers

Hydroelectric dam

How can a river power a town?

A river can power a town when it flows through a hydroelectric dam. The water passes through special machines that turn the river's energy into electricity.

River flows to the sea

How many oceans are there?

There are five oceans, but they all join together to make one enormous World Ocean. Most of the Earth is covered with oceans and seas – about 70 percent!

At rocky shores, rock pools form when the tide goes out

All kinds of animals live on a coral reef

What ocean animal is both big and small?

Coral is! It's a tiny animal that builds a rocky cup around itself, but billions of them together create a living rocky reef. A reef makes a great home for other animals too!

Why is the sea salty?

Salt in the sea comes from rocks on the land. Rivers bring the salt from the land to the sea. Some salt also comes from rocks at the bottom of the sea.

I'm a parrotfish. I nibble on reefs and make sandy poo. Golden beaches are covered in my coral poo!

The water in the World Ocean is always on the move, flowing around the Earth as currents.

Wind creates waves at the surface of the ocean

I'm a green turtle. I swim across oceans to lay my eggs on a beach.

I'm a mako shark – the fastest shark in the ocean.

How deep is the ocean?

Where the ocean meets the land, it is shallow. Further away it can be very deep, dark and cold. Strange animals live there!

Fangtooth

Angler fish

What is the Equator?

The Equator is an imaginary line that cuts the Earth into two halves. Near the Equator, the weather is hot and sunny most of the time.

Arctic Circle

NORTH AMERICA

EUROPE

I am a jaguar, and I live in the tropical Amazon rainforest in South America.

The Sun shines strongly around the Equator, and there is daylight for 12 hours a day, every day.

Equator

SOUTH AMERICA

I am an emperor penguin and I live on frozen Antarctica with lots of other penguins, seals and birds. This is the coldest place on Earth!

Where does the Sun shine at midnight?

During the summer months in the far north of the world, the Sun doesn't set. In places such as Canada, Alaska, Russia, Greenland, Norway and Sweden the Sun can be seen in the sky at night. But in winter it is cold and dark all the time.

I'm a polar bear, and I live in the far north on the Arctic ice. I love eating seals!

I'm a tiger and I love the rain. I live in tropical forests of India, and I'm a very good swimmer.

ASIA

AFRICA

What is a rainy season?

Tropical places near the Equator are hot and humid. Strong winds called monsoons bring wet weather in summer. This is called the 'rainy season'.

OCEANIA

ANTARCTICA

How many?

1 The number of years it takes the Earth to travel once around the Sun.

24
The number of hours in a day... because it's the number of hours it takes for the Earth to spin once.

365
The number of days in a year.

About **50** volcanoes erupt every year on Earth.

One of the thickest blankets of snow ever measured was **9** metres deep. That's as tall as three elephants standing on top of each other!

The sea freezes over near the North Pole in winter. The ice can be more than **3** metres deep in some places.

The deepest part of the World Ocean is called the Mariana Trench. It's about **10 km** deep!

2 The number of summers enjoyed by Arctic terns every year. These white birds fly all the way from the Arctic to the Antarctic to get the best weather!

In one year, **10,000** millimetres of rain can fall in a tropical rainforest, while less than one millimetre falls in the driest deserts.

It takes about **1000** years for a drop of water in the World Ocean to flow once around the Earth.

1.3 million Earths could fit inside the Sun.

In the Antarctic, around the Earth's South Pole, temperatures can drop to **−50°C**, or even lower.

Earth is about **4.5 billion** years old.

In the last **50** years about one third of all Earth's rainforests have been cut down.

No one knows how many different types of animal there are on the planet, but it could be as many as **10 million**.

Are all deserts hot?

No, a desert can be hot or cold, but it's a dry place because it rarely rains. More rain falls in the hot and sandy Sahara Desert than in Antarctica, which is a frozen, windy desert that's covered in snow!

Hoodoos

Pillar

Arch

Why do desert rocks look so weird?

The wind picks up desert sand, and blasts it against the rock. Over time it carves out some amazing rock shapes such as hoodoos, pillars and arches.

Why do I need such big ears?

Those big ears help a fennec fox lose excess heat in the Sahara Desert. They're also good for listening out for burrowing bugs under the sand.

Why don't penguins get frostbite?

A penguin's body is suited to life at the Antarctic. Its thick feathers are like a waterproof blanket, and warm blood travels through the bird's feet so they don't freeze.

Penguins hold their eggs on their feet to keep them warm

Oasis

What's an oasis?

An oasis is a place where water can be found in a hot desert. It's one of the few places that plants can grow.

We're Bedouin people. We live in tents so we can take our homes with us when we travel to find an oasis, or food to eat.

Does it rain every day in a rainforest?

It can do! Rainforests are found in tropical areas around the Equator. The Amazon Rainforest is the largest rainforest in the world. It's in South America and is home to millions of animals and plants, from tiny ants to giant trees.

Monkeys and parrots feast on the tropical fruits

Why are plants important?

Animals need plants to survive because plants make oxygen. It's in the air, and we breathe it. Plants are also food for us and many other animals. When plants die they rot and turn into soil, which we use to grow more plants.

Rainforest plants have giant leaves and they grow flowers all year round.

The forest floor is home to fungi, frogs and billions of ants and other bugs

Trees grow tall and straight to reach the sunlight

It can be noisy in a rainforest. Birds sing, insects buzz, and howler monkeys like me call and whoop to each other!

Lizards and snakes hunt insects

Silent jaguars creep through the dark shadows or hide high up on branches

Morpho butterfly

Lianas are climbing plants that have long, bendy stems and dangling branches

Would you rather?

Would you rather search for aliens in **space**, or travel to the bottom of the **sea** and discover freaky fish?

If you were frozen water, would you prefer to be a **snowflake** or an **icicle**?

Would you prefer to be as tall as a **mountain**, or as colourful as a **rainbow**?

Would you rather swing like a **monkey** or swim like a **fish**?

What type of boat would you like to be in right now...

...a canoe on the **Amazon River** or a sailing boat on the **Atlantic Ocean**?

Would you prefer to dig for **diamonds**...

... or **dinosaur** bones?

If you lived somewhere else would you prefer to live in the desert like a **fennec fox**, or in the Arctic like a **polar bear**?

If you could be a plant would you choose to be a giant **rainforest tree** or a prickly **cactus**?

What do we get from the Earth?

We get lots of things from the Earth! They are called natural resources. Animals and plants are used for food and clothing. We use metals and other minerals to make things. We can even use wind and water to give us power.

Plastics are strong and waterproof. They are often made from oil, which comes from the remains of tiny animals that once lived in the sea.

Glass is made from sand

My bike is made of different materials that are found on Earth.

Rubber is a bendy, stretchy material that comes from rubber trees

Rocks are made of different materials called minerals. Metals such as gold and silver are minerals. Most sand is a mineral called quartz.

Metal

Fossil

Some fabrics are synthetic, which means they are made from oil or other chemicals

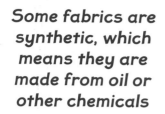

Pencils and paper are made of wood, which comes from trees

Rubber trees

Metal is hard, shiny and strong. It doesn't bend easily. Metal comes from rocks that were made in the Earth's crust.

Sheep fur is called wool and it is used to make fabric

Some fabrics are natural and they are made from plants or animal fur

Diamonds

Where do diamonds come from?

Diamonds are a type of mineral that forms deep below the Earth's crust. Diamond is the hardest natural material, but it can be cut to make sparkly precious crystals or 'stones'.

Why does Earth need our help?

We are doing lots of damage to our planet!

We chop down too many trees. But trees make oxygen for us to breathe, and are home to many animals.

We poison the oceans with waste. Coral reefs and animals die in dirty water.

We pollute the atmosphere. Dirty air is making our planet too warm.

So what can YOU do about it?

Recycle your rubbish instead of throwing it away.

Turn off water when brushing your teeth.

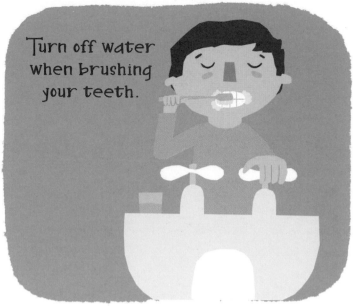

Let your computer sleep instead of screensaving.

Don't leave chargers plugged in at the wall.

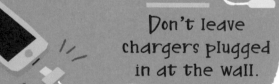

Pick up litter!

Plant trees!

Get involved!

Happy Earth Day!

On 22nd April every year, people across the world take part in activities to help make our planet a greener place.

A compendium of questions

Why don't we fall off the planet as it spins through space?

Thankfully, a special force called gravity keeps us on the Earth. It's a type of 'pull' force and the Earth, being heavier than us, pulls us towards its centre.

How does walking help the Earth?

Most cars and buses use fuel made from oil to power their engines. They make air pollution, so it's best to walk, or cycle if you want a healthy planet.

Can cars run on chocolate instead of petrol?

Yes! Chocolate comes from cacao trees and it can be turned into a type of fuel called biofuel. Biofuels are cleaner than petrol, so that's good news (but a terrible waste of chocolate!).

Why did my bike go rusty?

Bikes are made with a metal called iron. If iron gets wet (when it rains) the oxygen in the water joins with the iron to make a new material called iron oxide, or rust.

Rust is an orange-brown colour

Can snakes live in the Antarctic?

Most of us live in hot, tropical places.

There are no snakes in the Antarctic – snow and ice make it too cold. Snakes keep their bodies at the same temperature as the air around them, so they would freeze to death. They need warmth!

Why do planes fly above clouds, not below them?

When planes fly, air pushes against them as they move forward. This is air resistance. Air is thinner above the clouds, so there's less resistance, making it easier to fly, and so use less fuel.

Will the Earth last forever?

Earth has been around for 4.5 billion years already but it's still very young for a planet, so there's no need to panic!

I'm still just a teenager planet!

How do people travel to the deep oceans?

Explorers and scientists use special underwater ships called submersibles to travel thousands of metres down. Only three people have ever reached the deepest point, in the Mariana Trench.

What is a tsunami?

It's a giant wave that hits land and destroys everything in its path. At sea, the tsunami isn't too high, but as it nears land, the wave may be 30 metres high. It's caused by an earthquake under the seabed.

Early warning systems allow people to reach safe areas, away from the coast, before the tsunami arrives

What time is it at the North Pole?

It can be any time you like! During the deep winter there is no day, and in the middle of summer there is no night, so 'time' doesn't mean the same thing at the Poles!

Always time for ice cream though!

Are there mountains under the sea?

Yes, huge mountains called seamounts. They are formed by undersea volcanoes erupting. The waters around them attract many different sea creatures as there is plenty of food.

How big is an ocean?

There are five oceans and they are all HUGE! Together, they cover two thirds of Earth's surface.

NORTH AMERICA

ATLANTIC OCEAN

> An ocean is a large area of salty water. It's also called the sea.

PACIFIC OCEAN

SOUTH AMERICA

> Seaweeds are plants that live in salty water.

Day octopus

SOUTHERN OCEAN

Long-snouted seahorse

Are the oceans important?

Yes, billions of animals and plants live in them! People use the things that live in the ocean for all sorts of things, too. A type of seaweed called red algae is used in peanut butter – it makes it easy to spread!

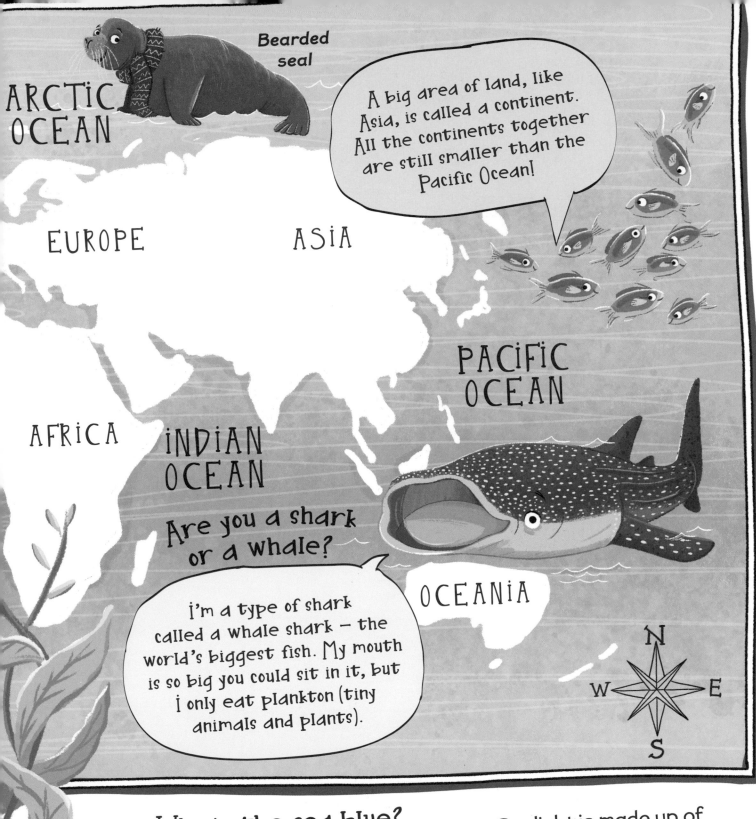

Bearded seal

ARCTIC OCEAN

A big area of land, like Asia, is called a continent. All the continents together are still smaller than the Pacific Ocean!

EUROPE

ASIA

PACIFIC OCEAN

AFRICA

INDIAN OCEAN

Are you a shark or a whale?

I'm a type of shark called a whale shark — the world's biggest fish. My mouth is so big you could sit in it, but I only eat plankton (tiny animals and plants).

OCEANIA

N
W   E
S

Why is the sea blue?

Sunlight is made up of lots of colours. When it shines on the ocean, most of the colours disappear into the water, but blue light bounces back, so the ocean looks blue.

What is a fish?

Fish are animals that have skeletons, gills and fins. There are more than 32,000 types, and most of them live in oceans.

Tail fin swishes from side to side when swimming

Overlapping scales are smooth and slippery

Herring

I'm the perfect shape for swimming. My silvery scales help water to flow easily over my skin.

Slim, sleek body moves quickly through water

Can people breathe underwater too?

No – sorry! You need to breathe air because you have lungs. All fish have special organs called gills that work in water.

Water and air have oxygen gas in them. All animals need oxygen to live.

Oxygen-rich water flows in

Triggerfish

Water flows out over the gills, where the oxygen passes into the fish's blood

Do fish have special homes?

Some do. Clownfish live among the tentacles of stinging sea anemones. The fish are covered in special slime that protects them from stings, but animals that might want to eat them can't get close!

I can glide for up to 200 metres.

Can fish fly?

No – but some can glide. Flying fish have very streamlined bodies and use their big fins to launch out of the water into the air.

Whoosh!

How is my nose like a shark?

Most fish skeletons are made of bone. Shark skeletons are made of cartilage, which is softer than bone. Our noses and ears have cartilage – that's why they're bendy!

Bull shark

Did you know?

A **hairy frogfish** is a fast eater. It sucks food into its mouth like a vacuum cleaner – 50 times faster than the blink of an eye!

At 3 metres long, the ocean **sunfish** is one of the world's biggest bony fish.

Octopuses can turn red when they are angry.

Electric rays can zap fish with an electric shock. Once the fish has been stunned, the ray can eat it!

Seaweed is often used as a thickener in ice cream!

The **sperm whale** has the biggest brain on the planet – and probably the whole Universe!

500 million years ago the only living things on Earth were in the ocean.

Baby sharks and baby seals are called **pups**, and baby fish are called **fry**.

Shark skin feels like sandpaper. It is covered in tiny bumpy scales that help them slip through the water.

I'm more like a hippo than a herring!

Whales and **dolphins** aren't fish – they are mammals.

North Pole

A **great white shark** can eat enough meat to make 3000 burgers in one go, and it won't want to eat again for at least ten days.

Polar bears and **penguins** never meet because penguins live near the South Pole and polar bears live near the North Pole!

It's like looking in a mirror!

South Pole

Sailors used to think that **dugongs** were mermaids. They're actually plump mammals that spend their time grazing on sea plants.

Do trees grow in the deep sea?

No – but giant kelp seaweed grows in huge forests! It is found in the Pacific Ocean, and can grow up to 50 centimetres in one day.

Bumps contain air that helps the kelp to float

A kelp forest is a great place to hide – one strand can be more than 30 metres long.

We are lizards that live on the Galapagos Islands in the Pacific Ocean.

Who picnics at the bottom of the sea?

Marine iguanas do! They dive to depths of 12 metres – and stay there for up to an hour while they nibble on seaweed that grows on the seabed.

Do baby fish go to nursery?

Young fish and reptiles keep away from predators in special hiding places called nurseries. Shallow waters around sea grasses and mangrove tree roots make good nurseries.

Sea otters can wrap themselves in kelp so they don't float away

Mangrove trees grow at the coast, with their roots in shallow salty water.

Sea creatures sometimes mistake plastic floating in the ocean for food. If we eat it, it can kill us.

What do turtles eat?

Green sea turtles feast on fields of sea grasses that grow underwater.

Baby turtles hide from sharks in the sea grasses

Who plays hide and seek?

Many ocean animals do! On coral reefs, millions of sea creatures live close together. Lots of them use clever tricks to avoid being eaten by the others.

I look like seaweed. I'm a type of fish called a leafy seadragon.

I'm a sea slug – aren't I beautiful? My lovely colours tell animals that I am poisonous.

I'm a decorator crab, and I'm holding onto a piece of coral as a clever disguise.

I'm a cuttlefish and I can change colour in a flash.

Do fish need friends?

My best friend is a busy little shrimp. I'm a coral grouper and my friend cleans my teeth.

I also nibble away any dead skin. Yum!

We moray eels have long, thin bodies and can hide in cracks in the coral. We eat almost anything we can catch.

Can you see a reef from space?

Yes! The Great Barrier Reef stretches over 2000 kilometres off the coast of Australia. Reefs are built by tiny animals called polyps. Each one lives in its own rocky cup, waving its tentacles in the water.

It took thousands of years for polyps like me to build the Great Barrier Reef.

How long does it take to make an island?

If a volcano erupts on the seabed, it can make an island in a few years! Lava (a type of liquid rock) pours out and builds up to create a brand new island.

Volcano erupts on seabed

A cone shape of lava forms on the seabed

The cone grows so big it breaks the surface – it's a new island!

Can I find treasure on an island?

Yes – but not the sort that belongs to pirates! The treasure to be found on islands is all the precious animals that live on them.

We're baby hawksbill turtles. Our mum laid eggs in a nest and then swam away. Now we're hatching.

We're leaving our nest and heading to the sea.

I fly to islands when it's time to build my nest and lay eggs. I'm an albatross, and I'm huge.

Black and white ruffed lemur

Christmas Island, near Australia, swarms with millions of red crabs. We lay our eggs in the sea.

Who lives on an island?

Islands are often home to animals that live nowhere else on Earth. About 60 types of lemur live only on the island of Madagascar, which is in the Indian Ocean.

Giant tortoises like me are found on coral islands in the Indian Ocean. We can live to be more than 100 years old!

How many?

About **100 million** sharks are killed by people every year.

I'm one of the longest animals ever!

10 metres The length of a bootlace worm.

400 million

The number of years that sharks have lived in the oceans.

There are more volcanoes under the sea than on land! **452** are on the edges of the Pacific Ocean.

Pufferfish have poisonous flesh. About **30** people die every year after eating them.

7 metres

The length of the biggest saltwater crocodiles.

A single one of my teeth can be more than 10 centimetres in length!

A starfish can have more than **30** arms!

There were **40 million** crabs on Christmas Island – until yellow crazy ants arrived. They spray the crabs with acid and eat them, so far killing about **15 million** of them.

My arms are covered with hundreds of tiny feet. I use them to walk on the seabed.

507

...the incredible age in years of a clam that was found in the Atlantic Ocean.

40,000

Phew!

...the number of eggs a herring can lay in one go.

A narwhal's giant tooth can reach **3 metres** in length.

350
The number of types of coral that live in the Great Barrier Reef.

That's why it's important to cut down the amount of plastic you use, and to recycle it.

1 million seabirds are killed every year by plastic rubbish that is in the ocean.

Who sleeps in a muddy bed?

Sea cucumbers do! These slug-like animals live in mud, eat mud and poo mud! Sea cucumbers are animals, not vegetables, but some people do like to eat them!

I'm a longnose sawshark. I hunt fish and crabs that are hiding in the mud. My nose is lined with sharp teeth!

The bottom of the sea is covered in mud and sand. It's called the seabed!

How do people explore under the sea?

People can't breathe in water, but we still find ways to explore the deep ocean. We can scuba dive, use submarines, or send robots with cameras.

I'm a glowing jellyfish called a mauve stinger.

Remotely operated underwater vehicles are one way for people to explore deep water from the safety of the surface

Who stands on three legs?

Tripod fish have three long, leg-like fins to stand on the seabed. Each fin-leg can be more than 50 centimetres long! Then they keep their mouths open and wait for food to swim right in.

Who lights up the deep, dark sea?

Sunlight can't reach the bottom of the deep sea. So some animals make their own light instead!

Viperfish like me use flashing lights to attract little animals to swim close. Then we swallow them up! My mouth is so big I can swallow animals bigger than me!

123

Which fish ties itself in knots?

A hagfish! It's covered in slippery slime and ties itself in knots when it is feasting on dead animals at the bottom of the sea.

Tying myself in a knot can also help me wriggle free of a predator.

How smart is an octopus?

An octopus can work out how to open a jar to reach food inside! It uses its suckers to grip shellfish and rip them open.

Can I drink seawater?

No – it can make you sick. Seawater is too salty, and often dirty too. The dirt is called pollution and it's bad for all living things.

Did that fish's eye just move?

Maybe! Baby flounders have an eye on each side of their head. As they grow, one eye moves to join the other – so the adult flounder can spend its days lying on the seafloor.

Why is a blobfish so ugly?

I'm prettier underwater!

When a blobfish is brought to the surface of the sea its soft, spongy flesh goes floppy. When it is busy hunting in the deep sea it looks quite different.

I live at great depths, so humans very rarely see me!

Which fish uses oars?

The fins of the strange, ribbon-like oarfish look a bit like oars. It's the longest bony fish – reaching up to 11 metres.

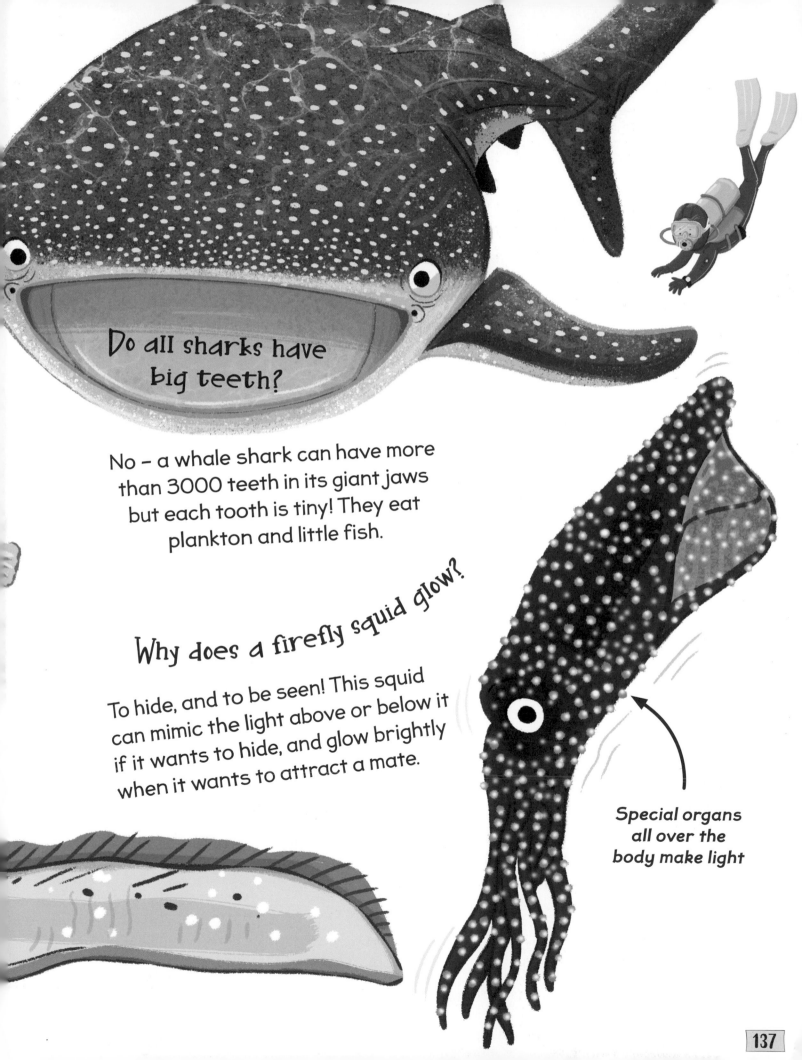

Do all sharks have big teeth?

No – a whale shark can have more than 3000 teeth in its giant jaws but each tooth is tiny! They eat plankton and little fish.

Why does a firefly squid glow?

To hide, and to be seen! This squid can mimic the light above or below it if it wants to hide, and glow brightly when it wants to attract a mate.

Special organs all over the body make light

index

A

aeroplanes 83, 104
air, effects of 57, 62, 71, 72
air resistance 104
    see also drag
albatross 119
Amazon rainforest 88, 94
Andes mountains 83
animals
    food chains 60–61
    habitats 76, 79
    navigation 83
    numbers 91
    oceans 86–87, 108–109
    rainforests 94–95
    spreading seeds 47
Antarctica 88, 91, 92–93, 103
Apollo spacecraft 57
Arctic 89, 91, 97, 109, 128
asteroids 13, 31
astronauts 29, 33, 72, 77, 82
Atlantic Ocean 57, 108
axis of Earth 18–19

B

baby fish 113, 115
bamboo 56
bar-headed geese 79, 83
bats 79, 83
beadlet anemone 124
bees 82
beluga whale 129
biofuels 102
birds 61, 79, 91, 119, 121, 126
    see also penguins
blobfish 136
blood vessels 49
blowholes, whales 132
blue whale 127, 132–133
boiling point 69
box jellyfish 131
breathing 46, 110, 132
buoyancy 66–67

C

carnivores 61
carrion 61
cartilage 111
cells, body 48, 54

clams 121
cleaner fish 117, 127
clouds 71, 84, 85
clownfish 111
colour 49, 59, 80, 109
comets 31, 33, 37
continents 57, 109
Copernicus, Nicolaus 28
coral reefs 86, 100, 116–117, 121
crabs 116, 119, 121, 132
craters 27, 30
crazy ants 121
crocodiles 120
currents, oceans 87
cuttlefish 116

D

day
    on Earth 18, 90
    on Jupiter 21
decorator crab 116
deep sea 90, 104, 114–115, 122–123,
    136
density 67
deserts 92–93, 97
diamonds 99
dinosaurs 57, 72
disease 44–45
    see also illness
dolphins 50, 113, 125
drag 62
dugongs 113
dwarf planets 13, 21, 33

E

Earth 12, 18–19, 22–23, 76–105
    centre of 20, 56, 83
    craters 30
    distances 33
    life on 32, 36–37, 76–77
    naming 38
earthquakes 78, 105
electric ray 112
electricity 52–53
Enceladus, Saturn 38
energy 52–53
Equator 19, 88–89
Europa, Jupiter 37
evaporation 84

Everest, Mount 79, 82
experiments 44
eyes 49, 136

F

fabrics 99
fennec fox 92, 97
fever 54
firefly squid 137
fish 110–115, 120–121, 126–127, 128,
    130–131
    coral reefs 86, 117
    deep sea 114–115, 122–123, 136
    density 67
    giants 133
floating in water 57, 67
flounder 136
flying fish 111
food
    disease 44–45
    ocean creatures 114–115, 117, 125
    plants 46–47
    poo as 73
food chains 60–61
forces 62–63
fossil fuels 53
freshwater 84–85
friction 63, 64
frogs 94
fruit 45, 47

G

Ganymede, Jupiter 20
gas 67, 68–69, 71, 72
gas planets 13, 24–25, 40
germs 54–55
giant creatures 119, 132–133
gills 110
giraffes 60
gold 83
'Goldilocks Zone' 36
gravity 39, 62–63, 64, 66, 71, 102
Great Barrier Reef 117, 121
great white shark 113
green turtle 87, 115
Greenland shark 128
grey seals 125
grouper 117
growth, plants 46–47

H

habitats, animals 76, 79
hagfish 135
hairy frogfish 112
Halley's Comet 33
hammerhead shark 131
helium 16, 25
herbivores 60
herring 110, 121
Herschel, William 25, 28
Himalayas 79
hippos 61
hydroelectric dams 85
hydrogen 16, 25

I

ice 37, 70, 81, 83, 90, 96
icebergs 56, 129
icefish 128
illness 54–55
    see also disease
Indian Ocean 109
Indian stonefish 130
iron 103
islands 118–119

J

jaguars 95
Japanese spider crab 132
jawfish 126
jellyfish 123, 131
Jupiter 13, 20–21, 24, 37, 39, 40

K

kelp seaweed 114
Krakatau volcano 51

L

lander spacecraft 34
lava 118
leafy seadragon 116
lemur 119
leopards 79
light
    deep sea 123
    direction of 59
    on Earth 80–81, 82
    speed of 48
    see also sunlight

lightning 39, 81
Lind, James 44–45
lions 60–61
liquids 68–69, 72
lizards 95, 114
longnose sawshark 122

M

magnets/magnetism 56, 63
    Earth 83
mako shark 87
mangrove trees 115
manta ray 133
Mariana Trench 90, 104
marine iguana 114
marine scientists 126
Mars 13, 21, 23, 32, 34–35, 36
matter 68–69
melting point 69
Mercury 12, 21, 22, 28, 32, 39
metal 67, 98–99, 103
meteorites 30, 56, 71
meteors 30
methane 25
minerals 98
monkeys 94, 95
monsoons 89
the Moon 21, 26–27, 38, 41
    days to reach 48
    landing on 33, 57, 77, 82
    tides 71, 124
moonbows/moonlight 82
moons 12, 20, 32, 37, 38
moray eels 117
mountains 78–79, 82, 83
    undersea 105
mud, seabed 122–123

N

narwhal 121
natural resources 98–99
Neptune 13, 20, 24–25, 28, 32, 33
night time on Earth 76
North Pole 70, 77, 82, 90, 105
nurseries, fish 115

O

oarfish 136
oases 93

oceans 86–87, 108–137
    deep sea 90, 104, 122–123, 136
    growth of 57
    pollution 100
    salt water 84
    size 108–109
    see also seas
octopuses 112, 127, 133, 135
omnivores 60
orbiter spacecraft 35
orbits 19
orcas 125
oxpeckers 61
oxygen 110

P

Pacific Ocean 108–109, 114
parrotfish 86
Patagotitan 57
peacock mantis shrimp 130
penguins 88, 93, 113, 126, 129
periscopes 59
pineapplefish 126
planets 12–13, 15, 22–27, 34–35,
    38–39, 40–41
plankton 109, 137
plants 46–47, 76, 77
    meat-eating 56
    oceans 108, 114–115
    rainforests 94–95
plastics 98, 115, 121
plates, Earth 78, 82
Pluto 21
polar bears 76, 89, 97, 113, 128
poles, Earth 70, 73, 76–77, 82, 90,
    91, 105
pollution 100, 102, 135
polyps 117
poo
    as food 71
    bats 83
    coral reefs 86
    sea cucumbers 122
    seeds 47
pufferfish 120

R

rainbows 38, 59, 80
rainforests 88–89, 91, 94–95

'rainy season' 89
ray fish 112, 133
recycling 101
red crabs 119
reflections 58
reproduction, plants 47
rings, planets 20, 24–25
rivers 85
robot spacecraft 34–35
rocks 98
roots 46, 49
rover spacecraft 35
rubber 98
runners, plants 47
rust 103

S

Sahara Desert 92
sailfish 127
salt, oceans 84, 86, 135
saltwater crocodile 120
sand grains 49
Saturn 13, 20, 21, 24, 37, 38, 39
scales, fish 110
science 44–73
scurvy 44–45
sea cucumbers 122
sea eagle 126
sea grasses 115
sea otters 115
sea slug 116
seabed 122–123
seabirds 119, 121
seals 125, 128–129
seas
    exploring 96, 104, 122–123
    ice 90
    salt 86
    tides 124–125
    see also oceans
seasons 19, 29
seawater 135
seaweed 108, 112, 114
seeds 47
sharks 87, 109, 111, 113, 120, 128, 131,
        134, 137
    teeth 137
ships, floating 67
shrimp 117, 130
sinking in water 67

skeleton, fish 110–111
sky, Earth 38
snakes 95, 103
snow 81, 90
snow leopard 79
solar eclipses 21
solar power 53
Solar System 12–41
solids 68, 70, 72
sound 49, 50–51
South Pole 70, 73, 76, 82, 91
Southern Ocean 108
space, sound in 50
space rocks 31, 37, 72
space stations 28
space travel 96
space walks 29, 50
spacecraft 34–35, 39, 40, 41, 57
speed
    of light 48
    of sound 49
sperm whale 112
starfish 121
stars 17, 41, 48, 70
    see also Sun
Sun 12, 18–19, 39, 41, 70, 72, 83
    Equator 88–89
    forming 14–15, 16
    life on Earth 77
    size 17, 33, 91
sunfish 112
sunlight 23, 46, 59, 80, 82, 109
swim bladder, fish 67
synthetic fabrics 99

T

theories 44
thresher shark 134
thunder 49, 81, 82
tides 70, 124–125
trees 49, 95, 100–101, 114–115
tripod fish 123
tropical forests 88–89, 91, 94–95
tsunamis 105
turtles 87, 115, 118, 134

U

undersea volcanoes 105, 118, 120
underwater sounds 50
Uranus 13, 20, 24–25, 29

V

Venus 12, 21, 22, 32, 39
Vitamin C 45
volcanic rocks 57
volcanoes 51, 78, 83, 90
    undersea 105, 118, 120
vultures 61

W, Y

walruses 127, 128
warm-bloodedness 70
water 71
    floating in 57, 67
    for life 37
    percentage in body 48
    sinking in 67
    sunlight on 23
water cycle 84–85
water power 53
water vapour 84–85
waves 125
Weddell seals 129
whale shark 109, 137
whales 112, 113, 127, 129, 132, 134
white beluga whale 129
wind power 53
year on Earth 19, 33, 90